SUMMER

Poems + Prose

CISSY STAG

Copyright © 2026 Cissy Stag, Stag Legs
Publishing

All rights reserved.

Dedication

For my pets... because I've grown tired of humans... and you're always there to dry my tears.

Introduction

Hi. I'm Cissy. I began writing this fourth book of poetry and prose in Summer of 2025, and I'm calling it a wrap in Spring 2026. I developed post-traumatic stress disorder about three years ago. Seasons carry a heavier weight than they once did. This book is about starting over in a new place... rooting down... and still finding myself heartbroken... but for the first time in years, I know that my home is safe. What a blessing it is to have the freedom to grieve.

Summer: Poems + Prose

Table of Contents

The Heat

I'm not agoraphobic. I just never want to leave
my house.

It's not fear. I swear. It's the heat. I detest it.

Maybe that's why I am the way I am-

always gazing into a little piece of glass,

waiting for a new hit.

I mean hint...

Something to light up my brain.

Wouldn't it be funny if you weren't real

outside of this tiny glass box,

glued to my palm like a sixth digit?

What if you were in there...

just... looking back?

Would your point of view

feel anything like this?

No Concern

It's of no concern to me
that I did not fulfill my potential.
How could I?

As a child, I didn't know
I was different
but not exceptional.
Creative
but easily lost in thought.
Drawn to things
my peers never craved:
Not a career.
Not a happy marriage.
Not children
or a house with a fence.

I didn't know
not until I hit rock bottom
that my deepest hunger
has always been
autonomy

of mind

of body.

Yes, I'm controlling

but only of myself.

Obsessed

but only because

I love myself

with ferocity.

Possessive

of my time

my energy

my resources.

Loyal to my core.

And always

learning to choose myself

the way any man

would do without shame.

The Farm

There are days that I cannot believe

that any of this is real.

This quiet place of reprieve.

Far enough from the city,

but not too far to disappear forever.

It's strange, isn't it?

How we grow used to chasing labor

and call it The American Dream?

"Do not envy thy neighbor,"

or whatever the damn book said.

For they tend the farm...

and me?

I just get to watch.

The Haze

On nights like this, I don't ache for sobriety.

I don't meet my eyes in the mirror and feel shame for the haze.

Pour Baby...

I should be ashamed, right?

I made it back from the abyss,

only to spend my days

sipping cabernet.

What do I even do

with bonus time?

I could stop anytime.

Sure.

Pour out my glass

and hope it's still magic

when I pour out my heart.

But what if I like my addictions?

Greige

It doesn't feel right, does it?
The sea is flat.
The ground is cold as stone.
You're dressed in white,
but the world stays greige.

Who would've thought?
That having everything
everyone else wants
could make you fade.

Sensitive Subject

I've become hyperaware of my own scent, my texture, my nearness to the air just beyond my fabric. It's hard not to be, especially when sex becomes the subject, and those who have never seen my flesh call it disgusting, while those who have touched it call it a mistake. It's hard to enjoy touch when what I really want is love, but I'm too impatient to wait for a love that might never come. So I try, in bursts, in borrowed moments. But when the affection ends, it's like it never happened. You never felt me. I never felt you. And in your absence, I don't miss your body. I miss your mind, your voice, the way you danced with me like I wasn't something to survive. So yeah, I'm on high alert for my most sensitive subject. It was never a fair offering.

The Bridge

We didn't burn it.

We just let it rot.

If we return,

will we find peace

or fall through a broken plank?

Let's say it still stands,

just strong enough to hold us.

Would we celebrate the crossing?

And when we part,

will we remember it kindly,

or stare at the water

and think about jumping?

Raindrops

Daylight breaks.

I shuffle to the kitchen-

three pills, washed down with tap water.

A soft nudge at my feet:

my rabbit.

I bend to give light head scratches

and remember,

even in sadness,

even in grief,

my life now is good.

Settled.

I return to bed without shame,

listening as raindrops tap

against the metal siding

of my mobile home.

Lift You Up

I hope you don't mind

when darkness consumes you...

That you don't look at my palm

and think my reach is meant

to steal your light,

instead of

to lift you up.

Okay?

Baby girl,

is it okay if I fix your hair?

Scratch your back,

hold you while your tears flow freely?

Is it okay

if I rock you like my own

though time has named you grown?

Will you let me care for you

the way you've always deserved?

Inner Thoughts

Something's off with you, my girl.
What's been on your mind?

You gaze back at me through golden light
and say, "I'm fine."

I shake my head

Deny.
Deny.
Deny.

I wish I could say that I'm surprised
but I've seen the original
and this is the reprise

You look like art in your glass box
They're loud, you know, your inner thoughts

And if the mask should ever fall
would you still recognize yourself at all?

I miss her...

I don't miss the $521-a-month car payments or the $2,500 mortgage split with my then-husband. I don't miss spending my life answering phones, preparing professionals for losses that so often came. I don't miss being hypervigilant, hyperreactive, or relied upon by others as if I were their spouse too.

But I miss the old me. The girl who danced every day and dusted her lids and cheeks with sparkles. I miss being able to draw a gaze like Bambi. I miss me before my eyes went dead.

I miss having hope in a career and creating without being bothered by the mess.

I miss when I liked Olivia Rodrigo simply because I liked her music, not because I felt her pain.

I love my life now, but I think about her often. I think about the girl whose trajectory could have been completely different if only she had been allowed to be herself.

Cheese

It came easy tonight. The heat of the moment. The excitement. The sex. Being held. And the sex again. We laughed.

"Ask me anything," I told him, and he asked me if I liked cheese... and then he named every cheese that came to mind.

I shared a handful of funny stories from adulthood and childhood and asked for his embarrassing stories. He shared his trauma, and I called him a sociopath.

It was warm. Uncomplicated.

I dreamt of you last night...

You showed up at my childhood home...

I was still living there with my mom.

You and I were both adults.

You asked if you could come in, and I said yes.

We chatted like friends do.

When it was time for sleep, you lay on the floor with just a blanket.

I asked if you wanted to sleep in the bed with me.

You said that you weren't sure if it was a good idea, but then you crawled into bed with me anyway.

We chatted for a bit more, and then you leaned in to kiss me.

I met your lips with softness and care.

My hand was on your thigh.

I moved my hand to cradle your face and accidentally grazed your intimate region.

I apologized. You said it was okay, and asked if we could go somewhere more private... where my mom might not catch us.

I said yes.

You began to shake.

I looked away for a moment, and when I returned to meet your gaze, you were gone.

A knock at the door came. A young woman said she was there for you and that your dad was waiting in the car.

I watched as you snuck out of my closet, where you had hidden to make the call.

After you left, you called and said you'd never see me again.

'"I'll never see you again either," I responded... a little too cheekily because I knew it wasn't true.

The Seafloor

Maybe it was the thrill of being swept off my feet that returned me to the sea

Always a swimmer

Never a runner

But even a swimmer is no match for a riptide

So I settle below the surface while the deep pulls me under

Back to my abode on the seafloor

Collecting shells and cups and kitsch

Do you like this painting of an iris?

I brought it from above.

I made sure I didn't lose my grip as the current carried me down.

Truthfully...

I don't feel closure.

I still feel like we are in collapse.

It's disappointing, ya know?

That we couldn't spare a friendship despite the ways that we decided to not grow closer.

Not risk it.

I weep.

Because fighting wasn't enough to dissolve the tether...

Running each other off wasn't enough to spare me the feeling of loss.

Grief.

In your absence, I'm learning to cope.

I always knew that it wouldn't be easy.

Test You

I want to test you.

Push your boundaries.

Stress test your mind until it is at its limit...

And keep pushing.

Until you snap like a Pixie stick,

And your sugar flows freely into my mouth.

Tell me...

What makes you happiest?

Dance?

Comedy?

Painting?

Writing?

Tell me.

I want to inhale your scent...

While we both quiver with desire.

Jealous

I got jealous.

THERE.

I SAID IT.

OKAY?

How could I not?

I was not jealous of her for fucking you when you were drunk.

I was not jealous of you because you were still unhappy.

But yeah.

I got jealous.

Because if given the opportunity to have me...

ALL OF ME.

Mind.

Body.

Heart.

Soul...

Why would you pass that up...

For someone who you definitely do not love?

Repel

Do you feel relieved?

To have been repelled,

And know that we are not running from each other?

Always a swimmer.

Never a runner.

Dive headfirst into the life you deserve.

You've spent enough time treading water.

Yours... not mine.

Do not try to force my hand on this issue.

My body is not up for debate.

Do you feel that between your legs?

I do.

Power...

Power to move forward.

Power to be shameless.

Unbreakable.

Desirable.

Worthy.

If I am your guilty pleasure,

The guilt is your burden to carry.

I was built for pleasure.

Tonight

Tonight, I weep

For the version of me that was fumbled by every lover...

Because I always had the most to offer...

Even when it didn't look that way on the surface.

Loyalty.

Peace.

Rest.

Sex.

Kisses.

Affection.

Back scratches.

Dance.

Song.

That look... you know the one...

A car.

A home.

A plan to live.

I love you, but I love me more.

Perfect Image

Does it matter if it's entirely real if it leaves you breathless anyway?

You know what I mean.

That feeling.

That look.

The things said without speaking.

Is it so bad to romanticize the way that things could be if the idea brings you to life?

Called Coffee

In your absence,

I feel compelled to write.

You told stories...

But I tell stories better.

grumble

I love you...

You get that..

RIGHT???

I do not want you...

But I want to see you happy.

Call me crazy.

Call me contradictory,

But don't call me anytime soon.

If I'm T-rex because I terrify you,

You're a fossil because you're old.

I don't want to use you anymore.

I got what I needed.

A muse.

A lover.

A friend.

A mortal enemy.

Someone unforgettable... who I loved so deeply that they became a part of my identity...

Farewell to my muse.

I will not miss you or the ways that you make me angry.

Or sad.

Or confused.

But I do wish you the best...

And maybe...

I will not miss you so much...

Because while I had you in person...

That wasn't the only way that I had you...

cough...

Whatever... I don't care... but I could.

Ruin

I could be the love of your life,

But I'm pretty sure that you'd ruin it every time.

Always a swimmer.

Never a runner.

You bled my heart,

And claimed your pedestal.

What does it feel like to be a winner?

Beau 🐇

Have you ever searched for love in someone

because they complemented your aesthetic?

I have.

His coat matched my throw pillows...

And that was enough for me.

Still Here

I couldn't help but think of you tonight,
driving through the darkness,
invigorated,
singing Lana Del Rey,
Summertime Sadness.

My windows were down,
my hair blowing.
All I could see were red taillights,
red like the city the night that we drove.
Pure blaze.
You riding shotgun,
me playing Chappell for the first time for you.

Does it bother you when I talk about it?
Do you even remember?
No one would know.
Just us.

It's the peak of summer,

and you're not here anymore.
How about that?

If you were here,
we'd grab a coffee tomorrow.
I'd tell you about the new Superman movie.
It was so cheesy.
I think you would've loved it.

You probably would've seen it alone,
somewhere in Midtown,
and kept cracking jokes,
comparing yourself to Superman from Temu.
I'd make fun of my enemies,
call them Lex Luthor.
And it would be fun.

It would be funny.
For us, at least.

Tonight, you're on the West Coast.

In some ways, you couldn't be farther,
and in some ways, you couldn't be closer.

I wonder how you'll react,
the day you come back
and realize I'm still here.
Rooted.
Just slightly farther away.

I wonder how you'll find me one day.
Settled.

Style

I hope that you don't grow to resent me out of shame...

Shame for growing attached to me.

But if you did, I'd understand it.

I felt that way once.

Hated myself.

And hated everyone around me.

Just because I was... abnormal.

Tell me why... in the presence of good company,

I still feel incurably lonely.

Call me anxious.

Call me fearful.

Call me dismissive.

Call me disorganized.

Call me avoidant.

Just...

Call when you can.

Scraped

I feel happy...

Almost, anyway.

Happy to no longer run.

No longer hide.

To be known.

Who.

Where.

When.

Why?... eh. We still don't know that one.

And know that my data will not turn to daggers.

Anxiety Nap

Is it okay if I rest my head here?

What if I miss a day of blue sky after my eyes drift shut?

Is this a life worth living if I'm rarely conscious for it?

Am I lazy?

Am I guilty?

Am I worthless?

Is my value only contingent on how hard I'll chase a dollar?

Back in '23...

I touch myself to the sound of my life falling apart.

I can still smell the crisp air of Carolina.

Feel it.

My body,

nearly bare on freezing nights.

Always in motion,

glitter on my eyelids,

sweat between my thighs,

back pressed against steel.

Do you remember it?

Falling in love when you shouldn't,

sinking,

deeper and deeper into the delusion

until it swallowed you whole.

Always searching for breath between tears,

and wondering,

is it over now?

Friends with Benefits

In your absence,

he looks at me like I used to look at you...

You know the look...

He touches me like you wanted to touch me...

Wide-eyed and full of adventure.

Hope.

In your absence,

I grieve a little less for our connection.

One that burned bright before eventually
burning out.

Call me crazy.

Call me a liar.

Call me soon?

Let's chat.

Like ex-lovers do.

Faith

It's strange, isn't it?

That I live in this world

Absent of a God...

But I still believe in you.

What does the magic feel like?

I should have asked,

but I didn't

because I didn't think I needed to.

The b!tch is SO back...

Baby girl,

This life is worth living.

Even on the days you cannot dance,

Or even stand.

When no one laughs at your jokes,

And you choke back tears.

Even if you grow fatter and older

(which you will, if you're lucky),

this life is worth living.

The world will change,

and so will your body within it.

So if you ever lose your joy,

do not lose your hope.

Because one day, things will turn,

and you'll be glad you stayed.

Annie's Town

I often forget how far I am while seated at the foot of Appalachia.

If I returned to The Triangle to review my old life,

would I be in awe that it was ever mine, or in complete disbelief?

Let's say I took the same trek down to Florida.

Eight hours.

Walked the coastline.

Visited Mickey.

Would it feel like home?

A vacation?

Or just a footstone to the end?

Despite not even being thirty-three, I feel like I have lived a thousand different lives.

Here.

There.

Always voyaging for a place to rest.

And then, one day, it appeared to me.

The place I would forever call home.

Annie's Town.

Not quite Atlanta.

Not quite Birmingham.

I struggled to accept its peace...

because peace never felt attainable.

But then I look up.

I see the moon over Annie's Town,

a moon I have watched many nights before,

from anywhere in the world.

And I feel anchored.

Hazel

Have you ever searched for love in someone

just because they matched your aesthetic?

I have.

His irises matched my headboard,

and in time,

the words ceased to lift the weight off my
heart.

Because I remained fixated.

His irises matched my headboard...

they were just hazel...

and that was enough.

Still Fixated...

At what point do I accept it?

That I won't get over you?

I tried.

Over and over and over.

A new warm body in my bed every time we fought.

I tried to stop loving you with reason.

You didn't love me back.

Or if you did, you never told me.

That should have been reason enough...

Right?

Wallflower

I'm sorry that I didn't consider the feelings of a stranger who dare not introduce themselves as I wrote my way through Hell and back. I should have been more considerate of a wallflower like you.

Atlanta Utility Works

Your absence is felt in warm, coiled light.

There's a sickness in your mind.

You should get that checked out.

Fold

I sometimes worry I will fall out of love with
you,
when the novelty of your naivety fades.
That you will always be outraged at the world,
performing as if you do not know better,
even though you do.

I worry that, as the years pass, your views will
bend toward what earns the loudest applause
instead of toward becoming a better man.

Why do I worry for you this way when you do
not worry for me at all?
Why expect you to fulfill potential when it has
been over a year since you called?

I should not fear falling out of love, but I do.
Because on days of gray and days of blue,
I dream of sharing my time with you.

And in your absence, if I am not spending my
time longing,
I simply feel lost.
So loving you in this way seems worth the
cost.

Because loving you helps me stay,
and gives me something to hold,
though my body is weary and ready to fold.

Sonnets (...this one's too short to count)

Can I smoke you out?

Roast marshmallows with you over a fire fueled by my sonnets?

Call a boy while we giggle...

Make him drive us to your dad's house...

And just toilet paper the place.

From branch to basement.

Would that be okay?

Could we lie on the cold ground with only fallen leaves to keep us comfort?

Could I kiss you?

Take a drag?

And kiss you again?

Kudzu + Sweetgum

Let's go to the store and admire the view on the way there.

Sunset and slick roads.

Kudzu and sweetgum.

Low beams.

Sweet dreams.

Simple fun.

Nemesis/Goddess

Green girl,

I don't blame you for your envy.

Spearmint

You chill my lungs like spearmint.

Underwater

No one sees your weeping underwater.

Rich

I want to write myself into fortune,

But gold seldom rains on the self-published.

Rich with love...

They say that's all that a poet needs...

Love.

Juliet (does not wear pants on her front porch)

"O Romeo, Romeo, wherefore art thou, Romeo?!"

I drunkenly call from my front deck.

The stars shine bright.

The bats settle into twilight.

For a trailer park, it's quite a sight.

Romantic, even... a double-wide delight.

Heflin

The kids a town over toilet papered the local police...

Oh, to be young and wild and free...

Ice Cream

Vanilla boy,

Can I splatter you in red, yellow, blue...

And call you Superman?

Eh... maybe Superman from Temu?

Overstimulated

Who is screaming loudest tonight?

The frogs?

The cicadas?

Or me?

Mashed Potatoes

Here sits Cissy Stag...

In a vat of mashed potatoes.

Because the world insisted that she wasn't an artist.

Didn't work hard enough.

Didn't spend enough money.

Bad at business.

Obviously.

A fraud.

A failure.

But it really isn't true.

People are just people,

And Cissy creates regardless of if it makes her a profit (it doesn't).

Call her life a lesson that you do not have to live yourself.

She failed.

You didn't.

But that's okay.

At the end of the day, Cissy knows that she is lucky.

Because she continues to create what she wants.

Even if it's just a self-portrait...

Plopped down in a vat of mashed potatoes...

The Economy of Unpaid Ambition

All work and no play when you're a woman in a male-dominated hobby.

Always a power struggle.

Punch down and pray that I don't punch in,

Grap a mop,

And clean the floor with your insecurities.

Does it matter, really?

I think not.

Rub your pennies together,

I'll take you for everything you got...

It ain't much because you're poor like me.

My dick this...

Your dick that...

At least we know I'm joking when I say that my dick never falls flat... (I'm cis...)

Complex Minds

I never imagined that there would come a day when imagination became controversial.

When day dreaming would be viewed as maladaptive.

When the dreams at night would be nothing more than sex and gore.

Are my thoughts even mine to have at this point?

Or are they just talking points for the next saga of performative outrage?

When did live and let live get thrown out the window?

Does not judging a book by its cover ring a bell?

No meet and greets when it comes to love.

Just fuck and ding dong ditch.

Who even cares if you're a poet?

It's clearly the least interesting thing about you.

Complex minds... made to be tested... not to be embraced.

That's what it feels like anyway...

Her House

I wish you could have seen the look on his face...

Heard the change in his tone...

The day that I showed him my phone...

And there you were.

Present.

Under a mask

With your opinion of him...

Clear as day.

"Move on," you told me.

"You deserve to be happy."

I wish you could see the look on his face...

As he realized that what I'd been telling him was honest.

Cautious Discretion

Have you ever searched for love in someone because you had a lot in common?

I have.

His irises were brown - like mine... but not quite amber,

And we'd lived in many of the same places.

Taken vows that were eventually broken and said that it was no one's fault.

It just didn't work out.

His irises were brown, and he seemed to have a mind like mine.

Smart. Established in routine. Witty.

...but... he wasn't a poet.

Or a writer.

Of if he was, he didn't think it important to disclose.

Much like he didn't think it important to ask about my poems.

And with one quip about my sanity,

I was simply done.

I cried about it hours later.

Because I've searched for love in someone's aesthetic... in their irises... in the ways that we are similar... yet different...

And I still haven't found a love worthy of my investment.

Not since the last one.

Bullshit

The words landed like a threat.

Until they didn't.

My guard fell many times

With many moons.

So much so that you'd call bullshit if I called it a mistake.

No regrets.

Just a pattern.

In this life, we may never shake hands.

If we don't, we really didn't need to anyway.

It would just cause a spectacle.
Probably...

...allies...

That's the best way to describe it now.

Replicas

It's strange, isn't it?

To spend a regular Tuesday creating a new galaxy...

Simply because you can.

Even after all of this time.

This must be what God feels like.

Buttercup

Punch down, buttercup.

You were warned before I punched in,

Grabbed my mop,

And cleaned house.

Punched out when I couldn't stay small.

If this is the Discord of Misfit Toys,

Then call me Big Bad because I won.

I huffed and puffed and nearly blew my brains out.

And guess what?

No Big Bag of Cash for the Big Bad of stand-up.

Funny, right?

Incantation

Lust for me.

My blood.

My body.

Love me when you know I'm tragic.

Feast on me,

You hungry sapphic.

Dream of me,

And keep it graphic.

Humid sighs.

Shaking thighs

Wrapped around your shoulders, baby.

Get me flustered.

It gets you hot.

To see me live the life you want

While blowing off the life you got.

Baby girl, I'll warn you now.

Your world changes when you break that vow.

Dream you may and dream you might,

Don't scream my name.

You'll start a fight

With the lover to whom you promised forever.

Speak my name not now. Not ever.

Creeper

I injected my pen with poison,

And you trusted me to etch it onto your skin.

Even as the words rejected your body...

Inflamed and bloody and covered in pus...

It was still a sight to behold.

Terrifying.

But beautiful.

Next time, is it okay if I tattoo the words *into* your skin?

Left hand... that's where you said you wanted your first... tattoo, right?

Wrapped around your finger?

Like ivy?

A little stitious...

Ten toes down on unholy ground,

But God it feels like Heaven.

Pick your fix.

I swear, no tricks.

Make your wish on 11:11.

We're a little superstitious in my world.

You would be, too,

if you rarely felt like a normal girl.

Meet me in wooded hills.

For sex and magic and spooky thrills.

Reminder...

Do you feel that rumble in your stomach?
Baby girl, you're power hungry. It makes sense,
after all... after being starved for so long.
Remember... a binge will make you ill... Your
anger need not be met with the defenses that
you learned last fall... and the fall before... It's
not better to be feared than to be loved. That's
just something that you believe when you're at
war with yourself.

Public Domain

Mirror mirror in a vault,

I'm trapped in a box, and it's all my fault.

Through wicked ways and feeble frights,

...exile may be my guilty delight.

QT

I've often found clarity in the rain, but sometimes rain is just rain, and while the moment is beautiful, you know that it is fleeting. There's a ball of anxiety in my stomach. The kind you get on the night before you go to Disney World. Visit Mickey and pals... I wake early, grab a burger from Waffle House, and mull on lovers' past. The rain begins while I'm in the diner. My previous muse is nowhere to be found, but I still feel included in the excitement of half the staff getting their uniforms soaked. I drive over to the QuikTrip... fill my tank... make myself a coffee and grab two bottles of orange juice... I can't tell you now whether the anxiety is present because my life will change forever... or because it won't. Maybe, I'll fall deeply... crash harder... write another book. Or maybe it will be an ordinary Sunday...

...

Cowboy, don't bring me a body and expect me
to bury it for you.

How It Ended

It ended like it began.

Sex.

A meal.

A drive.

Your hands around my throat while I gazed at you with a spark in my eye and a taste for danger.

We sang Beautiful Things... you smacked my thigh.

I screamed... and caught your hand every time after.

It was pain and pleasure,

But the ending with neither.

Just the end of a season and the acceptance of fall.

It was a relief...

For a summertime fling to be just that.

A fling.

Not a forever yearning.

New Lover

Fall came,

and so did a new beautiful man...

Three times, in fact!

Deepest Desire

...you know what I want? Not to say, "I love you," and pray for it to be accepted at a minimum... but preferably reciprocated. I want to be told, "I love you," and I want to say, "I love you too."

Collectibles

I should return them, really.

I don't need multiple copies of every book cover I've ever created just to tell myself that I put in the work.

But I think I'll keep them anyway...

Money is just money, and sometimes a reminder is needed of every time that I've banked on myself... even if it wasn't profitable.

Hidden Gem

I am often frustrated by my own brilliance and the way that it is overlooked... like a hidden gem - the kind you'd find in an overpriced bag of sand. Ripped from the mines and packaged for your entertainment only to sit amongst the other dirt bags through most seasons... eager that each summer will be their best yet...

Easy

It's Friday night, and I'm not drowning my sorrows in red wine or tequila and soda. In fact, I forgot that it was Friday until now. My mind has been preoccupied with what I said last night to my new muse… "I'm going to fall in love with you." I've given a few folks such a warning in the last year, and it has not panned out. I don't know why I feel the pressure to say it so early if I am not already in love… I think that I just need them to know that if they let me down, I must be let down easy. I'm fragile.

Beautiful Everything

It's a beautiful day, and I feel incurably lonely. My first thought as I woke was that I need a step-by-step guide about how to be well-liked. Because it's not enough to be funny. To be independent. To create beautiful things. To have a nice smile. Maybe it doesn't help that so much of my writing is sad. Or angry. Or euphoric. It's not enough to put myself out there to connect. I remain consistent - always a target for projection of other people's insecurities while I wear mine on my sleeve despite knowing that they will be exploited. What a beautiful life...

I Wasn't

I opened up last night...

To a man worthy of my time and affection

About why I am the way that I am...

And what I want going forward.

It wasn't easy,

But it was nice.

Safe...

I'm finally safe.

And then I rested.

Truly rested.

Foothills

We tiptoed on the borderline of each other's boundaries...

Until we realized that the earth below us would not crumble if we settled.

Look at us now.

I'm in the mountains.

You're in the city.

My, oh my,

Is the view up here pretty.

I Beg of You...

Love me wholly.

Love me when I'm unholy.

Love me through my folie.

Love me slowly.

Love me only.

Pick me from the meadow.

Leave your trace.

Cradle me.

My body.

My face.

Love me hard.

Love me soft.

Love me for what I cost.

Love me for being too much.

Love me because my too much is your just enough.

Incapable

Cry me a river, little wolf,

And I'll cry you a pool.

Invite you to swim laps,

Then belly flop from the high dive to get your attention.

Brace for impact

And let the chlorine fill my nostrils.

Cry me a river, little wolf,

And I'll tread in your tears bare naked

Just to prove that I'm a brave girl.

Immortal and incapable of sinking to the bottom...

Or so I'd like to imagine.

When you're away...

When I drink, I think of you.

So, maybe I'll finally stop.

Give up my vice and the wine.

Stop going back in time

Just to remind myself that you did me dirty.

Read Me

Tell me, my dear, how this thread untied from its spool.

Pick a deck.

Show me your cards.

Read me.

The Magician.

The Devil.

The Fool.

In My Bed

I sleep with the lights on to keep the monsters in my bed at bay...

But it doesn't stop them, ya know?

The dreams that are both lucid and tactile...

I kindly excuse myself from each narrative created by my own subconscious to find myself in a new scene.

Flying.

Falling.

Fucking.

The cycle is endless.

Wake to bide my time by daylight.

Return to my thrilling slumber and hope for rest.

...redo?...again?

I'm wondering what if again...

What if we could go back in time?

Meet.

Maybe become friends.

But never kiss.

Neither or us bare our bodies.

Or our souls.

If you could go back for the redo, would you?

Would you trade your life now for another shot to become anyone other than the perfect villain?

He Paints in Oil & Ink

I love the scent of sex and soil.

Biomorphic lover,

Paint my mind like the night sky - dark at the edge of my atmosphere.

My surface dressed in fog, heightening your senses as you absorb the echo of my calls.

Let me wrap you in the warmth of my core.

Don't flinch

I consume those I adore.

Fixation (is a curse)

In your absence, I continue to break my own heart with the thought of what if...

What if you don't think I'm pretty?

What if you don't think I'm funny?

What if you don't think I'm intelligent?

What if you think I use ChatGPT to write my texts to you?

(I don't. I'm a great writer.)

What if you think I'm in love with someone else, and I'm just not?

What if I pushed you away too early?

But also... what if I pushed you away too late...

just in time for me to get attached and find myself swimming in fear of your ambiguity?

Fixation is a curse, and I simply do not know how to fix it.

I stopped projecting my best qualities onto folks when I realized that they'd never live up to my idealism...

So, if I expect nothing from you, and I know why you are the way that you are... tell me...

Why do I still feel so lonely in your absence?

Misaligned (probably)

I wish I could say that it's fate.

I really do.

I wish that I could say that the stars aligned, but I haven't a clue.

I am too afraid to look to the sky,

So I look to the ground...

Watch my step.

Try not to trip over another lie.

I wish I could say I love you,

But I can't.

I never felt safe to love you.

No rhyme to it.

Just another statement I make in the name of art as my heart hardens and then crackles over your disinterest.

American Bronze

In his presence, I felt like I was floating in summertime.

He had locks of American bronze and irises like pebbles.

I was infatuated.

Strange isn't it... that I asked for his permission to fall in love?

I think we're breaking up...

I opened our texts to apologize for my abruptness - feeling like I'd been unreasonably cruel.

Distance doesn't feel safe for me.

Is it wrong of me to hope that you'd test my boundary just to let me know that you care?

But maybe you don't.

Maybe I want to reopen the line like I love to pick at a fresh scab.

What if this? What if that?

What if I ever felt safe enough for my mind and body to finally stop hurting?

...we are definitely breaking up...

I asked you not to contact me,

And I felt cruel with my request.

It's not that I don't like you.

I do.

A LOT.

But I couldn't handle the weight of constant interpretation.

Always wondering.

Is today the day that I show you something that makes your brain light up...

Like mine lights up at the receipt of your simple complaints?

And now I'm drunk again...

Walk with me up the street to see the mountainview.

The stars here are bright to everyone - not just to me when I'm feeling blue.

Please forgive my drunken swagger.

I struggled to find my footing before the booze hit my blood.

Walk with me. I'll tell you my worldview.

But please understand,

I share because I ache to be loved.

The Notebook

To love me adequately, you need to be at least a little bit crazy. Not dishonest or willing to gaslight me when I feel our foundation shake. Do not pick at my insecurities. That's a battle that you will not win. But you need to be a little bit crazy and a lot crazy about me. Noah to my Allie.

I don't think I can forgive you for that...

How much writing must I do for you to grasp the concept and hold me tightly?

Don't play dumb when I tell you I'm confused.

I asked you if I should leave before I got attached,

And you pulled me closer.

Eliot

I want so badly to reflect on our time together fondly - give me a reason to look forward to the possibility of you entering my orbit again one day... but the overwhelming memory I have is not of the fun we had or the snuggling together with your pets... the good sex... the food... or watching Robin Williams... the loudest memory is of every time you pulled away, and I doubted my own intuition about what was happening... we didn't even fight, and maybe that was a problem too. It is as if we interlaced fingers when we met and with every week that passed, each set of digits untwined... we were no slow burn... just slow to extinguish.

Cuffing Season

In your absence, I might be okay. Maybe we were never meant to be anything other than people who kept each other company during the loneliest months... but if that's true... why did I feel so lonely in your presence?

Talbot

The scenic overlook is eerie without the stray we named. His makeshift doghouse is long abandoned, and his bowls are full of dirt. Like us, he came and went. The trees once lit in gold, tangerine, and auburn have stripped naked. There is something hollow in this feeling - like it was a place I'd shared with you, but I truly hadn't. I sent you the photos, and you passed up the opportunity to meet me where I stood.

Godless

Split. Between faith and the real world. Faith in a love that will find me. Grow organically. What a tragedy to be a Godless being but still have faith.

What happens in Vegas always comes back...

You returned and with you came renewed fear that I'll return to my old ways. Put you on a pedestal. Call you my muse to compensate for not being chosen. Serve you my heart on a platter as if I don't need it to pump blood through my own vessel. And yet, with your return is newfound excitement. Because I finally feel like myself again... and losing myself to lovers who drink from my attachment wound has been quite the burden.

Intersection

I'm grieving us, and I really can't tell you why. I didn't fall in love with you... but maybe because you never gave me the green light to do so? In your absence, I just feel confused... not about you. We were over when you tactfully labeled me a friend after I stripped naked... body and soul... despite us not being friends prior. The fog settles over a heart and mind that aches with your memory but is relieved to no longer ask for your permission.

I'm talking to a guy on Hinge...

I don't mind the quiet of night, but it gets awfully lonely being the only warm body in my bed.

Oof...

You blew me a way. Truly. Call yourself a man.
I'll call you a magician. Because I've never seen
a man stick both of his feet in his own mouth
quite like you do.

Vroom, Vroom!

Meet me in Anniston.

I want to go to the races with you.

Drink overpriced beer that we both tolerate.

Feel the rumble of power through our flesh and bones.

Scream for a bunch of rich guys who risk their lives for our entertainment.

And imagine that I was the rich man behind the steering wheel...

I can trust you with this... right?

Baby girl, I need to tell you a secret...

Trust that my disclosure is in good faith...

Don't look behind my back.

Tisk tisk.

I trust that you'll take my word for it.

My fingers aren't crossed...

Swear on your grave and mine...

Oh...

There is no "what if" version of us that exists
on impulse...

What is there to lose...?

I've been mulling on yesteryear for a while,

And I think I'm finally ready to ask...

Do you want to try again?

Because I know that there is no answer that would break my heart this time.

There is no friendship to ruin...

Only friendly greetings of hello and goodbye as either of us exit of our own accord and wonder if it's a coincidence that we always leave in unison.

And even then, I don't think we could ruin that.

Nick

I'm ready to let go of being jaded by you. Have been for a while. We used to interlace fingers and dance. And maybe that's when I fastened my grip. White knuckled your disrespect and bandaged every cut to my dignity and reputation while believing that I could love you enough for you to stop taking aim. But you didn't. That's why I didn't ask if you wanted to try again. Because I don't.

JuDe

Hey Jude,

Your dude is still keeping me secret.

Maybe it's rude of me to tell.

But the alternate is to tell you both to go to Hell.

At this point, why not?

You deemed it fit for me through summer, fall, winter, and spring.

Here we are again - another cycle of him talking fame, fortune, cradles, and rings... while rejecting the notion that you two are dating.

Tonight, the ground will freeze, but Hell will remain the same.

Call me obsessive, desperate, and controlling for one more refrain.

He says he tolerates me, but I see the tears well as I tell him that we are not friends.

Just friendly acquaintances, and boy is that swell.

It seems reasonable, all things considered.

No apology now. No apology then.

And hey, maybe he justifies you like I justify James.

Please understand, our situations exist in separate lanes.

See how easy it was to lay it out?

No hem. No haw. No discretion devout.

Hey Jude, want to know a secret?

That's what girls do, right?

Look out for each other?

The secret is that you won

Him and all of his secrets.

Because believe you me... I'm done.

Swear on your grave and mine.

Palms wide open. No catch. No crime.

We shook hands on it, so it's fine... right?

My fingertips probably didn't give me away...

Certainly not as I brushed his wrist and wished him goodnight...

Sharpen the Blade

Your words were like whetstone... sharpening the knife that I used to cut the fruits of my labor. In your absence, I feel joy... and it feels normal... like I am biting into sweet flesh on a hot summer's day.

...so I had sex with your ex-friend and forgot it was your birthday...

I fell out of love with you,

And it was your fault.

I'll start by saying that.

Looking back, I'm not certain that the power of my love was influenced by your greatness...

Because you are no great man.

I think that I just wanted you to know what it was like to be loved.

Because you told me that you hadn't been.

Loved.

Picked.

But you had...

And you couldn't love her back either.

Tonight I balance on a rope of uncertainty...

About my own interests...

But I think that we're finally done,

And I knew that as I took the leap.

Knowing damn well that I betrayed no one

But that you'd say I did it to you anyway.

For my father...

Hey, dad.

It's me.

Melissa.

Going by my legal name, which you selected.

In honor of your date to prom.

A math teacher.

I tried to call you tonight, but you changed your number.

And that's all I really have to say.

Best of luck to you in your new life.

I pray, for your sake, that you are never subjected to the shame that you are indisputably worthy of.

Maybe you'll find happiness in avoidance.

In playing dad to a daughter much smarter than I am.

In becoming a grandfather to the children who I could never bear for you as I learned to prioritize my own health. And well-being. Despite always loving children so deeply.

I wish I could say without a shadow of a doubt that I hate you.

But I really don't.

Here's a song for you.

Because Bob Seger is your favorite.

And frankly, I have nothing more to offer.

I don't remember who this is about.

I fear that we keep each other at arms' length because we are sad people,

And blaming each other for our sadness is the easiest solution.

Thought it tonight as my tears formed perfect droplets.

Thinking about it now as imperfect rivers flow from my eyes and my nose.

I expected to be triangulated... again...

Everyone gets their karma, and sometimes their karma is me. Neither fragile nor unstable this time. Just an illusionist. I set aside my bag of tricks in good faith... but never forgot the contents as others showed me their cards.

Might be Andrew... might be Brandon... either way, it didn't work out.

I want to love you and it not be a lesson. My character is overdeveloped. I want to know should I ever bear your flesh and blood that I am free to tell you before I take the pills. That you'll understand or that I'll be so confident in you that I can choose the little dream, and we'd live it. And I wouldn't be alone. Again. I want to know that should I mother, I am not mothering you. Smothering you... because I don't know how to love half full.

Melissa

Baby girl, I need you to stop waiting on a person to lay your foundation for a life worth living. Your marriage will fail and so will every relationship after. The earth below you will shake for a while, but you will eventually find a place to bury your roots. He may dream of settling down in a place to share, but you will give yourself both the home and the garden while he remains displaced. Baby girl, your intuition is worth trusting. It will be your saving grace.

Filters

I think we've all been there... thrown a handful of sugar in a fire to watch it crackle with excitement... then just... wait... while the fire slowly extinguishes on its own. We fabricate The Magic to satisfy our curiosities. Our egos. Do you see this sky? It's alluring because it's pink... but it wasn't originally that way. It had shades of lilac... blue... orange... yellow... I tweaked it... just to know what it would look like... to answer the "what if"... but neither my creation nor the photo of the natural sky compare to Mother Earth's display of our atmosphere. I felt The Magic because I was there. Witnessed it with my own two eyes...

Weed

You're fragile like a dandelion, ya know? If I get too comfortable... plop down on a couch too hard... hug you too tightly... or exhale a sigh of relief, you just... vanish into the wind. Pieces of you are everywhere, taking root in yards and fields and sidewalk cracks. You're pretty... but I understand why they call you a weed.

Apathy is best served cold.

All is fair in love and war, and this is war.

It's a shame that we don't know what we're fighting for, but we do it anyway.

We use sexual expression and private information as currency... take aim, and discharge our weapons as we see fit.

And who cares that none of us are happy?

Time goes on, and so do we... repeating our patterns until they become undeniably part of our character.

I'd cry out of frustration if I could, but my sadness has been conditioned into apathy.

Because I know that we're at war... and we might be in love... so... all is fair.

Why should I care?

Look at me... begging again...

I didn't venture into The Hills to hurt you.

It just felt right at the time.

And then I feared you'd grow angry with me for what I'd done... and for what I told... and for how I enjoyed it...

Before your birthday.

I did not intend harm...

And I did not know how to say that it wasn't about you without sounding cold...

And that I'd just... forgotten.

Does that make it worse?

I don't check my calendar all that often.

I want to be angry with you because I think you may be angry with me,

But I'm not sure that you are.

I want to tell you that this is final, and in many ways, it is...

But I think that I will always have a soft spot for the man who lost my trust... he suffers like we do.

Dear Reader,

If you see Iris, tell him that I miss him...

And I guess that's all...

Piss in the Snow

Baby girl, take my hand.

It's okay that you're tired.

I understand.

I am too.

I don't always feel The Magic when I wake...

But I also stopped grieving at every daylight break.

I built the life that I wanted... and the world remained cruel anyway...

So maybe this is just how we cope?

No mask. No smile. Just dwindling hope.

Instead of growing angry, we grow numb...

To conserve energy... as we learn of crimes that cannot be undone.

Baby girl, I wish I could tell you that the end is near...

But I just don't think that to be true.

In the meantime, I'll do me, and you'll do you.

If I seem absent sometimes, I want you to know...

You are not alone.

Not in mind or body or soul.

Call it written in the stars or piss in the snow.
Baby girl, we'll get through.
No need to put on a show.

@lrustygussetdrive

She's moving in to the home that we shared with my old guitars and my childhood teddy bears. She'll sip her coffee and set it down on my father's cedar chest that he insisted I keep mere months before he decided he no longer wanted to be my father. Her linens will fill the drawers of the dressers I bought from the old lady who sold me my first house... our first house when we wed. She'll bond with our rabbit and love him like I did. Love you like I did. Her home an Autistic woman's paradise... because it was decorated by an Autistic woman. I even painted some of the things that hang on the walls. She'll settle down and settle in without having to remember how we fought... about... everything. The furniture. The yard. And even the house itself because you didn't want it when I did... and I convinced you to take a chance on it anyway. She'll park her car in the garage that you refused to live without in the spot where I used to park my Subaru that we fought about because it was more expensive than your Honda. When she tells people her address, she won't flinch because it won't remind her of when she was stalked by strangers. She won't have a panic attack in a Costco a state away when she fills her prescriptions. She'll have a happy life and be with the version of you that I didn't have when you insisted that I needed an individual therapist but you didn't. You'll get married, and you'll likely never get divorced. You'll grow old in the house together while I might not grow old at all. She'll never know what it is like to try to leave and to be held back... because she didn't get berated for dancing at her favorite gay bar. Or for covering the cost of brunch or groceries for friends. Or for quitting her job when it burned her out. But if it doesn't work out... I hope you let her go. Because as I picture her living the life I used to live, I don't worry that she'll enjoy the kitchen too much or love my rabbit better than I did. I don't worry that she'll read my books of poetry or play the piano that you used to complain was too loud. I don't worry that she will walk into the closet and run her fingers through the tulle of my wedding dress... or flip through our wedding album before going through my childhood CD collection and saying, "We should get rid of these." I worry that if it doesn't work out... that she doesn't have to file a petition citing the dates that you argued just so that you let her leave.

About the Author

Cissy Stag is the author of *Stripped*, *Tethered*, and *Wax*. She lives in Anniston, Alabama with her goth children: Echeveria & Beau (rabbits), Orin & Elizabeth (cats... Elizabeth is orange, though.)

www.ingramcontent.com/pod-product-compliance
Lightning Source LLC
Chambersburg PA
CBHW021544150726
47990CB00006B/2388